FEAR OF THE RIDE

FEAR OF THE RIDE

Ronna Bloom

HARBINGER POETRY SERIES
AN IMPRINT OF
CARLETON UNIVERSITY PRESS

Printed and bound in Canada

Canadian Cataloguing in Publication Data

Bloom, Ronna, 1961-
    Fear of the Ride: poems
(Harbinger Poetry Series; 2)

ISBN 0-88629-302-2
    I. Title. II. Series.

PS8553.L67F4 1996 C811.54 C96-90065-0
PR9199.3.B56F4 1996

Cover photo courtesy Canadian National Exhibition Archives
Author photo: Rick Zolkower
Cover design: Barbara Cumming, Carleton University Press

Carleton University Press gratefully acknowledges the
support extended to its publishing program by the Canada
Council and the financial assistance of the Ontario Arts
Council. The Press would also like to thank the Department of
Canadian Heritage, and the Government of Ontario through
the Ministry of Culture, Tourism and Recreation, for their
assistance.

 Harbinger Poetry Series, Number 2

for my family

ACKNOWLEDGEMENTS

My thanks to the editors of the following journals
where these poems first appeared:

The Antigonish Review
The Canadian Forum
CV2
Grain
McGill Street Magazine
Queen's Quarterly
WRIT

This book would not have become a reality without the
generous encouragement of Rhea Tregebov; the
presence of Judith Katz and Ruth Gilbert; and the
support of the Poetry Hot Line — those who listened:
Isabelle Zolkower, Mary Lemke, Karen Malis,
Lynne Mitchell, Jay Brodbar, Lisa Schmidt,
Falia Damianakis, and Chris Garbutt. Thank you.

I gratefully acknowledge the support of the Canada
Council. Thanks also to the Ontario Arts Council and
the publishers who recommended me. And thanks to
the Banff Centre for the Arts for the space to do it.

CONTENTS

The dashboard lights in our Dad's blue car
are warning red. Here, three hundred miles
from Thunder Bay. Drive to a station
everything blazing. Mechanic says: Lucky.
You could have burnt the engine. Cap gone.
Not a drop of oil. We look
at each other: dumb and young
thought we could drive that way forever.

WHAT A KICK FEELS LIKE

WHAT A KICK FEELS LIKE (I)

My sister tells what
the kicks felt like:
Not fluttering — what do doctors know,
they think it's eyelashes
waving inside your stomach —
gas, she says.

WHAT A KICK FEELS LIKE (II)

Blunt about birth.
My sister tells how
the body's sound changed
when she screamed
it's coming, it's coming,
then that low moaning and she knew:
Now it's coming. Hearing her own
voice from the womb, voice
pushing out.

NOTICE

March 28, 1987
5:05 pm
a girl is born. Fresh
from Montreal her grandfather
arrives, bringing bagels
and an indelible grin. Her aunts,
grandmothers return to the hospital
from The Pickle Barrel in a flurry
of Reuben sandwiches. Her father
flushed, on his feet by the bed, says
I wouldn't have missed that for anything.
Her mother lies back, the girl
curls into her chest, ten fingers,
ten toes. Such a girl. A present
for me, my birthday too: aunt
for the first time and I'm
taking her picture.

ONE MONTH

The baby is nursing but not gaining
weight. Her legs are bowed
thinner than birth.

The family goes to Zellers anyway:
colour photos flash on a bright
white ground. A doctor

enters their lives, speaks
certainty, statistics,
draws pictures. Maps

out three surgeries: two months, two years, then
five for complete sealing. Excellent
prognosis. My sister blinks

into his eyes. Of my own
roll of black and white film, the negatives —
our thin plastic proofs — remain undeveloped.

Up and down the side streets she is wheeling the stroller,
tears streaming up and down like streets. For days now
though no one has seen her. Since those diagrams sketching
all she couldn't see: a hole in the heart. She remembers
the last time she saw her blue car in the tow truck's rear
view mirror. Looked the same as always: same bits of rust,
same boxy self. How could she know from the look of it
something had stopped? And it was a car and old, god it was
probably fourteen. The doctors are upbeat, quote statistics,
but her tears don't stop. Just now she is heading down Marlee,
past the apartments full of young, single Jewish women
as she was so recently, so urgently. She turns left
takes Roselawn over the bridge. She rolls over the Allen
Expressway crying hard: not fair not fair not fair.
Her hands wrapped around the plastic piece, the stroller's
bonnet outstretched to prevent sun. She looks down as a car
passes and imagines a mistake: a car could come right now,
she thinks, and send us both over the wall into the highway
and we would both be dead. Now. She looks down into the
highway full of cars and stops crying, looks into the
bonnet. Takes her kid home.

MARCH 12, 1992

The men shovel.
Sound of crunch and fall.
The men in suits and gray faces dig.
The thin crust of March
clinging to trees.
The earth closing
one spoon at a time.
My father digs with his whole body, born
to this gesture.

MISSING

Someone cut off my arm
and for the first week
it was wrapped so well in blankets
I didn't believe it was gone.
On the eighth morning the blankets
removed, I walked
around the city block
raw nerve endings
nothing could cover.
You tell me
cry and the pain dulls
grow your hair long
to cover the space
and I do.
Sometimes while juggling
I forget it's missing
and then look down and see
nothing. And you know
it was my best arm
my new pink arm
I had just grown it.

THIS CLEAN

I go to a party, the last day sitting shiva. Everyone
a stranger. I look at men. Nobody tall. It doesn't matter.
I want a body, hide in the kitchen from the idea.
The word inappropriate comes in on a platter with toothpicks
and I go into the hall. There are men there too.
Everywhere there's combed-in musk and wrist bone.
Apples moving in throats. In the basement there are
fingers netting the air. I want to be that air. Want someone
to know I've been in mourning want no one to know I've
been touched. I'm clean. No one will be this clean again.
Death takes everything out of you. Put it back, put it back.
Everywhere there's fragrance, everywhere judgement.
Who do you tell you've just buried a five year old and
sex is on your mind.

HAND-ME-DOWNS

Three party dresses
fill one cupboard,
a life supply.
Two pairs of shoes
rubber boots.
You know everyone
she ever met. Hold
all the facts
of her four years.
Not much to hang on to.

BIRTHDAY

i Today is my birthday. I've spent it in a small space,
like a room with a chair and table.
I rode downtown in it, took it down Bloor,
went out for coffee in it, me in my room.

It was empty there, like the year itself
had been subtracted, surgically removed
like her.

ii Once birthdays could hardly contain themselves,
they lived inside ready candlewicks
like bombs someone had to light. They'd go off
with the extravagance of dream
and I, the diva of the day,
would grin behind pink glasses
a green smile of arrival, of waiting culminated,
of eclipsing order, overtaking older and younger
sisters at once, of poking out the day me my bomb
exploding for just this set of moments
like being sprung
from the middle: my name on the cake.

Today is your day.

iii On this day my sister had a daughter. And we had
4 days together and then she died and then birthdays
got smaller, went inside. So today
on Bloor Street, I carry myself around in something like
a room, passing people with matches in their pockets,
remembering light.

INSIDE

Will you come to us angry
from filling the hole
your sister left,
rising like a pumpkin in the stomach,
trying to revive us?

Our long longing wraps you, anonymous
inside, you could be anyone.

We imagine you a girl, another
space to pretend.

For you I offer this wish:
Be a boy. Not to have
her frozen photograph
mapped in your face.

Don't tell us the sex yet,
we need this dumb peace.

Meanwhile, your mother drops raisins
into her mouth, your siblings laugh
imagine you eating,
your face upturned
like a new bird.

i I lift up the phone and hear you
   not your voice but in the background
   behind the caller there's a faint
   beep   beep
   and I ask my friend
   can he hear the sound like a heart machine.
   It's my air conditioner, he says.
   But it's still there on the next
   call and the next caller says
   she can hear it too but goes on
   talking.

ii Your mother dreams you sitting
    with her smiling, the whole family
    can see you but no one else.
    Your father asks her
    what you said, what you said
    but it was nothing, only your
    big smiling, your hands
    in your lap, you were just sitting.

iii The other children speculate:
     she's doing somersaults, maybe she's
     doing cartwheels, maybe
     she's with God, or
     in Florida. Contemporary heaven.
     To be with Mickey.

iv I dream you for the first time —
We sit
with our arms around each other and sing
"Where do you want to be?"
and we answer together: different places,
but twice in a row
we say the same place
at the same time:
"I want to be in the country."
"I want to be in England."   —

I pick up my
phone and hear you, heartbeat
on the line

SUPPOSE

We're supposed to float together on a witchy cloud
over Toronto. Bake cookies, chocolate sprinkles
silver coins; take trips up and down elevators;
find the exact velvet dress you want
and you are supposed to let me buy it,
come home hugging it as though it were me.
We're supposed to run from room to room
in the Royal Ontario Museum naming birds,
find eggs, feathers, gummy nests
in drawers just at your height and you're
supposed to let me keep up but not get ahead.
We're suppose to eat ice cream at Greg's
watching ourselves in the mirror, watching
our tongues, supposed to take your
ever so much younger brother for a walk and you
get the apples because its your job and you don't
trust me to remember.
We're supposed to play a game in which you tell me
I'm dead and I die for you flat out on the couch,
waiting to be resurrected, by you, but you don't.
You're supposed to, but you don't.
You have me lie there while your brother, anxious
shakes my knees. You turn away indifferent
toward the house you're building, me
waiting for you to bring me back say —
I don't want to be dead anymore
and you're supposed to want me back, but you don't.
You're supposed to be seven now.
Supposed to be alive.
We're supposed to do something.
I don't know what, but we don't.

You arrive in the face of your sister
unexpectedly, in her eyebrows
when she is chewing gum, when
she is wearing a hairband. You arrive
and it surprises your mother to tears.
What could she say when she sees you?
What could she say? Your sister is
four. The age you were when you died.
Once you talked about a man who grew
older and older, deader and deader.
How did you know so much already?

Your brother has passed you
like a speeding car, like a tree. You will
always be older than him somewhere.

But you stopped at four, he was three, now
he's six and with every new grade he understands
you a new way. That you are not coming back
but, still, why? He asks
What can a person do in heaven?
Your mother answers, Anything they want.
If I were in heaven, he says,
I'd want to come home.

He seems to be all right these days
but when you left, he became the the oldest
with such a lurch, didn't have time to grow
into it, became an expert worrier. His rules
are strict, won't let me colour outside
the lines. He is careful. Lies down
on the kitchen floor when he's bored, his neck
thin as a spoon. He misses you.

You have another brother you never
met. He is curly. Maybe he's you too.
How bold of me to think
you never met him. What do I know?

Outside these lines, the language of daily
speech cannot hold you. We can
never say: She has two brothers, one sister.
Do the dead not have relatives?
To say: she had two brothers, one sister
means something happened to them, which isn't true.
Everyone's fine here.

How can we all fit into one
sentence? There is no tense for this.
Your mother, how many children does she have now?

You are in two worlds at once. If I
dedicate these lines to you, they float away.
If to your mother, they stay. If I send them out
in both directions, what confusion. What.

Let's spit
on the law of language that splits
us into then and now, there
and here, shout: You are dead, you have
two brothers, one sister, many aunts, I am one.
You have a mother and she has you.
You are completely dead and wise
beyond your years, however old
you are.

WHAT A KICK FEELS LIKE (IV)

My sister asks

> How much can the heart take.
> One muscle.

The first child
says to the second,

> You can have that toy now,
> Gillian's dead.

ORDINARY IS BROKEN

ORDINARY IS BROKEN

When ordinary is broken, love

at the funeral, the wedding, the car crash.
Hearing the sirens, cars part and people emerge
rushing up from their days, touch
the arms of strangers, speak

ordinary is broken like skin and love bleeds through
and everyone's shocked. Blood, we say.
Surprised to see it. Blood

quickly a bandage, another day
covers the wound love gapes
in the polluted air. Time heals
all love and go on from there quickly.
Everything open gets filled, gets closed.

SHE GETS DRESSED

A woman on the sidewalk in a nice suit
has two eyes a nose and a mouth.
The skin is bubbled, not her
original face. Her eyes look out.
She's waiting for a lift. She stands there
everyday. In a nice suit.

I imagine her going to be bed one night, trusting
the night and waking in flames,
waking in a hospital, in bandages, in a new face,
waking to scream
My House, My House, holding her face
waking up

And she wakes up
and doesn't look in the mirror. She has another
face. Not the one she spent 20 or 30 years with.
She looks out, sees her eyes and someone
else's face and she gets dressed, eventually
somehow.

ON THE MOON: 1961-1993

i I dreamt I was walking on the moon
no, floating. No gravity. Stuck.
Frustrated. I was frustrated on the moon.
Who gets frustrated on the moon?
Such a privilege to be there, to waste time
being frustrated.

ii You're on holiday and you come back
and people say — did you have a good time?
you were gone for two weeks.
Two weeks is life already,
who has a good time everyday for two weeks?
There are good days and bad ones
on holiday.

iii This man from the Sudan was studying in England.
He said: I know you. You've been on the road
for a third of your life. He said:
Hell is not a foreign land.
I thought he said, Hell is but a foreign land.
Later I knew: you carry it with you.

iv I dreamt I was walking on the moon
and it was fun, only I got stuck
and it wasn't the moon. It was
Treblinka. That crater.
I wanted to leave but realized I couldn't ever leave
as no one does,   ever,   leave. You stay to remember.
I thought it would be better if there were other souls around
like at a shiva house, where mourning
is a community.

v I dreamt I was walking on the moon.
This is where I live. I am not an immigrant or a tourist —
this is home. I was born into it, like a body. Only,
no one knows. They think I live in Canada.
Toronto or Montreal or even England. No one knows.
The moon. A quiet place. No sounds. No smells. No sense.
I carry it with me. The surface of its skin in my sides.

HERE

My friend Joe's been dead twelve years
he's used to it already.

Me, I'm scared to meet him after all this time.
"A-1 number 57, turn left at the oak."

Behind my lids his picture
fixes and unfixes itself

and I tell him I miss his softness.
You can have it,

he says.   Here.

TO FIT THE ABSENCE

The shirt collapses like a tent
its pegs removed. Water closes in
over the space a hand made.
Water has no memory.

Before the surgery you sing
love songs: 'I won't forget you'
and cry, talking to your left side
as though talking to a child.

You tell your breast it is going
to a better place, knowing
it will be cut up and thrown away.
Then you tell her everything.

You hold your breast on the subway
forgetting that women don't
do this in public.

Behind your breast your heart beats so fast
the doctors give you drugs to slow it down.
Behind your breast your heart
and without it now, your heart.

When we say good bye, you twist

hold back the gap
protecting emptiness.

But you can't.
Your heart is now more
clearly visible, closer to the surface
of your skin.

PROTECTING OURSELVES FROM WINTER

I was going home to help my mother sell her house.

We hit a truck.

We'd lived there for 27 years.

No one noticed.

When I got there all the beds were gone but hers.

The train just stopped.

My arms and legs got numb, I had to lie down.

We waited until dark watching the snow
then someone came to tell us what happened.

I just lay there.

I didn't believe it when he said
we hit a truck.

On the other side of her bed.

How can you hit something as big
as a truck and not notice?

My body stopped.

How the fuck can you hit something
as big as a truck

I couldn't move.

smash through it, splintering
it behind you

My sister organized everything.

and need someone to tell you
what happened?

She spoke to the movers in French, made them coffee
in the middle of the night. They were moving my mother
in a snowstorm.

How?

It was a positive move, everybody said.

The fuck.

My mother's first place on her own.

Can you not feel that?

THE LINEN NAPKINS

You left me
your linen napkins
folded
with the clean smell inside
ready for opening.
I'm afraid to use them
and lose their creases
as though you were held
in their perfect original folds
and will be lost with washing.

ISRAEL IN THE MOVIES

I flick on the TV and Paul Newman
in Exodus doesn't fit. Not
the Israeli I expect. Except
in 1960, the Jews were good guys —
men in fields, returning to a place
they'd never been at last
and Paul himself: ultimate here, prodigal son,
was always coming home.

Now in my living room, this movie moment
reveals its age, here in the dying
swelling strains of Hollywood
is the Israel of my indoctrination.

◆

I remember Hebrew school:

Trees planted in Canada Park
with our tongues, oh the stamps we licked
filled pages, each a small green symbol
of something growing somewhere.

The mandatory horror of reels and reels of bones
flickering in the gym. We lined up for those films
like something out of one of them — a long row of names
too big for us, growing into the past, trying on
the present, some distant country, supposed to be ours
again

again the music swelling, fragrant
the land's own lullabies
singing and singing
hair shivering on my neck —
I have lost this.

◆

Today on television Exodus
looks like America: where every true vision
gets bigger, goes to IMAX;
or gets insistent, goes to reruns
and forgets itself.

◆

Israel is a foreign heart inside my heart
forgetting home is the body, detaching itself
from its membrane, its memory —
forgetting me.

◆

In the remake, Exodus '93,
the Jews are bad guys
or at least, the fallen heroes
wearing history as armour, hardened
hard to like, to watch
so far across the screen

and Paul Newman is playing
his Arab friend, (from the original),
reinventing the hero
coming home.

HOPE

HOPE

You have a craving
it's the tongue's determination
you want a smoked meat sandwich.
Fat not lean, bread falling open to release
the meat. Your nose is sharp
your eyes are clear and scanning.
You go into a hardware store
ask for a smoked meat sandwich
fatty, and a coke.
They tell you they don't make them
but you insist, you know what you want
your tongue is not wrong
and you rail at the man in the shirt with the buttons
pulling, believing he's hiding them
in the back with the boxes of nails, bags
of salt. You can smell it on him. He's just
eaten one and holding back.
You leave angry, threaten
to return again.

You go into a laundromat, ask
for a smoked meat sandwich. Smell
of soap fills your nostrils and you suck in.
A woman looks at you not looking at you
and you swing around wildly
wondering where the kitchen is.

You walk down Spadina, notice a pickle
has rolled into the street, don't know
where it came from. The sick smell of fish
rides your throat. You look
at the pickle with hope and keep going.
Enter a chinese restaurant ask for a smoked meat
sandwich. They offer you noodles
and eggplant and you think
you are getting closer.
You try some and it tastes sweet
and spicy on your tongue, it makes
you cry and you leave.

Still you want a smoked meat sandwich.
You wonder if they make them in this city
maybe you will have to move, you've heard
there are such sandwiches on every corner
in Montreal, you can get what you want
24 hours a day in New York.

You walk south on Spadina
reach the fashion district.
Go into a clothing store
ask for a smoked meat sandwich,
and the woman at the desk apologizes,
says she has one
but not in your size.

THE CHAIRS

The chairs in my mother's house are perfect
papier maché chairs. Legs and backs with inlaid mother
of pearl, delicate and well preserved.
There's an illusion covering them like fabric, a voice
drawing you, saying — sit here, I'm empty.
But from some other place, deep within the seat,
my mother's mother whispers — sit here at your own risk,
sit here at mine. For though I am beautiful, I am
made of paper. Ancient skin. Sit here
like a lady. Do not spread.

And in I come to find my mother (my mother!)
in one of the more tolerant chairs, one with arms,
and she is wearing sweatpants and a T shirt,
looking out the window, one leg slung across an arm,
and nothing happens.
The chair does not complain or groan
doesn't wag the finger of its arm or crumble,
it just sits there holding her
no matter what she's wearing. It holds her
unlike any lap she's ever known.

A DOG'S LIFE

I took each small want and answered: *No. Go away.*
Each small and warm want that came wagging —
pantpantpant — I sent away: *Bad dog. Bad.*
Expecting it not to come back ever
but it did, came back this morning,
small beast that that it is, came thumping and moaning
back. No amount of stop your whining
can kill a dog, only flattens its ears
makes it feel ashamed if a dog feels shame.
A dog can't stop coming back, wagging its tail,
rolling in rotten fish and pissing on the floor.
Me, I thought I was different, could shut that dog down,
shut down having to depend on someone
to let you out, to not hit you or shame you.
Better not to want, better not to eat or move
or run, but to lie still.
But this morning, after the fine meal I had last night,
a strange meeting of the mind, two of us
wagging our heads off, licking life,
I woke up with that dog howling in my stomach and I
want.

She is bone thirsty and you are pouring into her and nothing stays.
Like a baby who can't keep her food down.
All you want it to do is be alive. Thrive.
The defeated feeding: nothing absorbed is ever enough.

Give up.

Your most courageous act is betrayal.
Find the line from your arm to hers that's draining off
and plug back into yourself, into your hum
and thrive.

Because your own blood wants to circulate in your veins,
because your own pump works, because your legs
exercise their right to walk, because
you are wired to stop dying.

And you watch from a safe distance, marbling
of pride and loss, jag in the belly button.

And you are here. And you are here. And you are here.

FEAR OF THE RIDE

I was always cautious or scared
avoiding the roller coaster
never took the Zipper or the Spider or the Flipper
just that low grade Tilt-A-Whirl —
never left the ground.

I was always being placed on a vengeful
horse who took me for a ride, galloped me around willy nilly
then stopped. And I'd be soaring
over his neck, landing like a rag, two halves of me
on either side of the fence and I'd be having to
Get Right Back On.

There were always these great sticks for skis
strapped onto my ten year old feet
and pushed from the tops of freezing mountains —
Go they'd yell
GO GO GO

And I'd always get a pain in my stomach or chest
a stay at home pain, stay inside.

And those people, the ones on horses or skis
or roller coasters had hearts
they wore outside their coats to show how much they loved
the sport, the ride, the chase, the steep steep steep.

Always these people showing their hearts, those outdoor hearts:
the ones young girls dot their i's with
or put through their ears, the ones they send
in envelopes. They flew there like flags or sails
so bright and breezy.

And all at once I gave up love
if that's how you had to wear it,
gave up the risk of moving fast
if someone else was pushing. In one fell swoop
I did away with hearts and rides. It was an honest death.

But now I want to play outside.
I want to look in the page of a pink pastel heart
and see myself throbbing there. I want
to get in a dune buggy without doors or roof and fly,
over sands not knowing when I'll stop
or if or why and keep going and fear,
ride the fear.   Ride.

FLIRTING WITH THE POSTMAN

We stand outside my apartment building, aiming
and flicking Canada Post rubber bands
into the wind, shiver with talk. We go into

the lobby's infinite space, in full view
of the neighbours, open the big envelopes
of ourselves, letting the words come out

unchecked. It's safe here.
We can always walk away. And do.
I say: I have to go up now. Or you move

on with your route, remembering
you're a public servant.
But something of us is stretching

beyond the lobby into our other lives. Something
elastic. And we don't know what of us will
hold, what will snap.

WHO IS THIS WOMAN?

Who is this woman thinking about sex,
repeating the words: big dick
to herself under her breath
the way a two year old told not to say a word
whispers it again and again.

She is getting louder in my mind
the words come to my mouth, almost come
out as the truth will
and I am getting wet walking down the street
even the word wet feels forbidden, a bad word.

Amazing how many bad words there suddenly are,
how many bad words become good.

All these bad bad words get new lives
years later in the mouths of other lovers.
Big dick. Big wet dick.

O the way they blazed from that kiln
glowing the red untouchables,
the way numbers in clock radios leap
into the dark, fill your eyes. Those pots
raised from the outdoor oven like embers on tongs:
shape of urn, of belly, red
shape of mouth. One illuminated bowl
held up to the sky, the welcome
spray of water hiss on clay and glaze
and glaze us over, us not knowing
what will surface
after so much fire so much water so much
colour and trust.

MARMALADE

Put to boil
six whole oranges unpeeled.

It's the orange
marrow makes
the liquid thick.
The stuff we can't see.

Like you and me
rolling in our thick
skins, these oranges
manage to breathe out
life, the sweet and bitter steam.
In spite of their cover, they make
the most alarming spread.

THE MEETING OF THE WEATHER

I felt the electrical storms
rushing around inside me,
the ones I'd been saving
every time I drove through them —
flicked into chaos
by your shining moon   your black
river eyes. We crossed a channel
in one breath
    a thin stream of eyes
the storm continuing for three hours straight
with and without rain
loud as the streetcar interference on the radio
the lights in my head all went
green   green   green
at the same time
and after you left
burnt out.

BREAKFAST

I've been revisiting that breakfast, unscrambling
eggs, returning the wilted spring
onions to the fridge and bringing back
to the mouth each said word
like a book read backwards
    lied you   angry I'm
like the tea being poured
up into the pot
everything reeled in.

I've been picturing that yellow cheese
which looked so fresh, til I turned it over
and underneath, saw the blue-green fuzz. You smiled
embarrassed by the moldy truth. You scraped
and scrambled at the stove hoping food
would make things right and oh,
what a cook you were.

The coffee was so good,
there was so much morning in the room, so much marmalade.
In spite of the Montreal bagels I love so much
I said everything
breathed out over and over and left
without breathing in.

TRANSLATION FROM THE SUMMER

Summer was another person
wide open, sleeveless
running.

Then winter (that dog)
comes and covers everything
buries its bones.

THE CITY

A network of roads spreads finely
through fields, between tower blocks
and building sites, it spins
through highways and downtowns
and downtowns. Dangerous neighbourhoods
await arteries. Maps
the city Toronto to the city Dublin to the city London.
All converge.
Circle road. Ring road.

I am going out all the exits on the highway
at the same time. Mapping
a leg to a shoulder, a memory to a hill, a blue vein
to an arm. Cross
sections of past. Yonge Street meets
Bloor north of Piccadilly Circus
like a skin graft. Major intersections
cross the body.

I don't know where I'm going and the city
calls to my voices, my limbs,
all my uncertain directions, saying:
Lie down in the not knowing.
Lie down in me.

THE WEEKEND THE SPRING

One day after a long winter of feeling slightly north of yourself,
your head and your body arrive in the same house
at the same time. The clocks move forward
but are exactly where they should be.
It is both 4 and 5 o'clock in the morning
and the sky is turning into birds.
You walk all day long in the turning
into spring time, carrying your jacket.
This long weekend, big enough to accommodate all its days,
is the weekend the spring comes back,
like a sleeveless shirt you never thought you'd wear again,
like a golden retriever.

YONGE STREET

I like the feeling of driving up Yonge Street
from the bottom at midnight
just me and the garbage trucks out this late,
the smooth flow of road without cars, river of street,
the blank shaft of sidewalk running beside me
like a dog unleashed loyal to the road.
No trees here or rocks, only restaurants
I glance in wondering —
Who's open this late? Who's left?
The garbage truck blinks up ahead
straddles the road
in only that way that midnight allows:
that spreading of self, unfolding limbs
and just plain taking   up   space.

The day is a dream now, with its —
DON'T WALK DON'T WALK commands
and — How dare you block
the longest street in the world picking up
garbage?

          I love
the secrecy of night,
swimming up Yonge Street, disobeying
rules of the day, winking the garbage men
passing them in the wrong lane
paddling the street like a quiet rapid
no one else watching. I am bold at night.
The street unpeopled invites me on up
dark and blinking
streams me home.

LANDLADY

My landlady was coming up from the basement, from the dark
cement underground where I've never been, where
all the incinerator shafts connect and collect the garbage.
She was coming up those steps, fat
probably two hundred and fifty pounds of her, full of all
of her self filled right out to the edge
of her skin, her long brown hair straight
down straight down past her waist past
her back, draped over her shoulders, straight
and swirling at the same time she was
coming up the stairs on a shell, floating
into the daylight out of the basement
on her slow feet I couldn't see them
for the concrete wall between us, she
was floating out of there like the Birth
of Venus, God she was beautiful.

THE JOB OF AN APPLE

The job of an apple is to be hard,
to be soft, to be crisp, to be red,
yellow and green. The job of an apple is to be pie,
to be given to the teacher, to be rotten.
The job of an apple is to be bad
and good, to be peeled, cored, cut,
bitten and bruised. The job
of an apple is to pose for painters,
roll behind fridges, behind grocery aisles,
to be hidden, wrapped in paper,
stored for months, brought out in the dry heat
of India and eaten like a treasure.
The job of an apple is to be
handed over in orchards, to be wanted
and forbidden. The job of an apple is to be Golden
Delicious, Granny Smith and crab. The job
of an apple is to be imported, banned and confiscated
going through customs from Montreal to New York.
The job of an apple is to be round. Grow. Drop.
To go black in the middle when cut. To be thrown
at politicians. To be carried around for days. To change
hands, to change hands, to change hands.
The job of an apple is to be a different poem in the mouth
of every eater. The job of an apple is to be juice.

CIRCLING

This is me.   This is you.
This is the sand at the beaches,
the french fries at the concert.
This is Ali Farke Toure, working
his rhythm into our bodies.
This is your finger, circling.

Fingers tell each other stories
minds only know partially,
and because they love to dance
nouns and verbs sway
waltzlike on our tongues.

The sides of our bodies rest
on the same seam of self
warm, in the night room. The gift
of lying quiet is unwrapped.

Crying has exactly enough room to stream
eyeless in the dark. Arms circle
breasts like wings.

A mind,
beaming and clear,
raised up on its petals,
on its trumpets,
announces a vision
of unity,
a preference for being touched on the thigh
with one tremulous finger.

visioning 39
viva voce exam 131–6

web sites 58
weekly review 5
word processing 124–5, 127

work packages 72–4, 121
work plan 74
Worker mode 4, 5, 8, 17, 20, 28,
  33, 45–6, 110–11, 117–18
writer's block 122–3
writing style 126–7

Index